BRIDE GROOM COURSE BOOK

DR DHEERAJ MEHROTRA

Made with ♥ on the Notion Press Platform
www.notionpress.com

Contents

Preface

Bride Groom Course Book*should be a priority for modern couples who are about to be married, particularly brides and grooms. As far as I am aware, there is no creative book geared explicitly toward newlyweds; therefore, I am confident that this endeavour of mine will significantly contribute to assisting all in-laws, brides, grooms, and relatives in being prepared for the pre-and post-wedding expectations. One of the pieces of guidance that we address in the book for the bulk of the readers is to "learn to fight issues, not each other." Open lines of communication, faithfulness, kindness, compassion, trust, emotional vulnerability, and a readiness to forgive wrongdoing are some essential components that contribute to the health of a relationship.*

Happy Learning as you enter a new stage of life with new responsibilities and ways of thinking about them.

Author

CHAPTER ONE

WHAT AND WHY OF MARRIAGE?

Marriage is a culturally significant and often legally recognized relationship between two individuals who are referred to as spouses. It is also known as matrimony and wedlock. In addition to establishing rights and responsibilities between them, it also does so between them and their offspring and between them and their in-laws.

People who get married take on the burden of caring for another person and being responsible to the partner they have chosen to spend their lives with. People who are married often lead lives that are more responsible, productive, and satisfying. This is because of both parts of the marital dynamic that are at play here. Because marriage is a formative event, it has the potential to change a couple's perceptions about themselves, one another, the future, and their position in the greater community.

Contrary to what many in Indian culture believe, there is not nearly as much of a need for it as they make it out to be. Don't stress out if you don't wind up getting married; you'll still have a wonderful life. As with religious practice, marriage is only a social convention, and people are free to decide whether or not they believe in it. If you do not believe in the institution of marriage, you have no need to feel ashamed about not acknowledging its presence in your life. According to Sadhguru, getting married should not be a duty imposed by society but rather a personal decision based on the necessities of each individual. Rather than being a requirement, getting married should be a personal choice. In addition, he goes into the correct etiquette for cohabitation relationships, divorce, and the actual wedding ceremony itself. The word "marriage" may have established a reputation for being connected with a very pejorative connotation because in many parts of the world right now, children have the sense of being free to do as they choose as they grow up. Young people in many different groups have a pessimistic outlook on marriage, seeing it as an undesirable institution that should be avoided. When you are young, your physical body is in a certain condition, and because of this, you tend to have a negative attitude about this situation. Marriage is an institution analogous to both a tie and a chain simultaneously. You have devised a detailed strategy outlining how to carry out the responsibilities. But as the days go by and the physical condition continues to deteriorate, you realize that you find yourself yearning, once again, that there was someone with you committed.

Either you get into a marriage, or you go beyond these aspirations. Neither option is viable. Both of these choices are unacceptable. However, this is something that each individual is responsible for assessing for themselves; specifically, the extent to which they are in need. If you want to look at this scenario with clarity and free from the impact of social variables, it is often recommended that you take some time off, say a month, to give yourself some space from the situation. Before making this decision, it is reasonably necessary for you to have perfect mental clarity. You must not in any way give somebody the ability to affect your judgment. You need to meditate and concentrate on bringing a certain degree of transparency to yourself to do this. When you find yourself in this condition of knowledge, it is essential to investigate how potent your demands truly are.

If you examine your circumstances and determine that marriage is not necessary for you at this point in your life, then that is it; once you have decided against getting married, there is no going back. If you have determined that you are going to go in a certain way, you should not turn around to look in the other direction. One of these responsibilities has to be completed by you in this session. If you spend an excessive amount of time in this transitional phase, you will discover that your state of mind does not alter at any point throughout this time. "Which alternative do you find most appealing?" There is no one object that can claim to be the most exquisite. Your life should be conducted in such a way that you should always devote your whole attention to whatever it is that you are doing at any given moment. If you possess this quality, it doesn't matter what endeavor you choose to pursue; you will be successful in anything you do.

CHAPTER TWO

How to be an Ideal Husband?

Reliability, emotional stability, and the ability to keep one's emotions in check are all hallmarks of a mature man. This indicates that he is probably resilient enough to deal with the difficulties, tensions, and disputes that come along with being married.

A strong, supportive, and intriguing partner who is able to weather the ups and downs of life with grace and endurance is a guy who has both of his feet firmly planted on the ground.

Find a guy who can deal with hardship with poise and dignity, rather than one who gives in to his emotions whenever things become tough. There's truth to the age-old adage that says, "A happy wife makes for a happy life!" (and the opposite is also true: "a happy woman makes a happy family").

Expressing gratitude to a person for their assistance might perhaps deepen your relationship with that person. Having a perception of one's own value is among the most essential components for happy living.

If you do not feel loved and appreciated by your boyfriend, you are taking a significant risk in your relationship. If your partner makes it abundantly evident to you, both in words and deeds, how much he values you, you can be certain that you will be content in your relationship with him.

Your flaws have to be tolerated in spite of his admiration for your qualities (such as being a wonderful chef, friendly, outgoing, enthusiastic, and supportive) (little messy, not so organised, talking a bit too much, not being on time).

At some point, he will have to come to terms with the idea that no one is flawless (including him). You are keeping your fingers crossed that he forms a favorable overall opinion of you.

Looking for a Photographer to Capture Your Wedding? No need to look any further. To assist you in making your decision, Vines of the Yarra Valley has prepared the definitive list of wedding photography businesses.

Ability to effectively manage disagreement is again a priority. In order for two individuals to develop a healthy and lasting closeness to one another, it is really important for them to argue with one another, disagree with one another, and have conflicts with one another.

Fights and animosity between spouses are major factors that lead to the dissolution of marriages. A significant number of other couples, in the vain attempt to lower the probability of having an argument with one another, avoid having meaningful conversations with one another. Despite this, strong communication is the foundation of a happy and healthy relationship.

A healthy relationship is characterized by the presence of the capacity to discuss disagreements in an amicable manner, free from the use of derogatory language or aggressive behavior of any kind.

A superb partner is a guy who is excellent at talking to you and who isn't hesitant to let you in on what he's thinking and feeling at any given moment. This kind of man has strong communication skills. Even if you and he don't see eye to eye on everything, he will still be able to carry on a meaningful discussion with you about difficult topics even if you disagree on certain things.

Trustworthy is a necessary trait, and to be able to trust one another in order to maintain intimate relationships. However, trustworthiness is a dynamic quality that requires a person to make consistent, intentional efforts in order to retain it via the choices and deeds that they themselves take.

If he lives up to his promise, demonstrates integrity, does the right thing when it matters, and is usually consistent with these attributes, then you may have found the man who will become your spouse.

You need not worry that he may put the information to inappropriate use or betray your confidence; you can be straightforward and forthright with him. You have faith that he will stay true to his promise and support your cause. You don't have any lingering concerns that he is deceiving you in any way, shape, or form. You have a deep-seated conviction that he cares a great deal about you and that he would never purposefully hurt you.

Make your relationship a top priority.
A significant number of the women I advise voice worries about their partners along the following lines: "I don't believe he cares about me or the relationship," "He stays at work long hours," and "He prefers to spend time with his pals rather than me."

It's fairly uncommon for married couples to have feelings of emotional distance from one another, despite the fact that they live together and have many obligations in common. They are no longer experiencing the same range of feelings or thinking at the same time as one another.

Successful couples work together to arrange delightful events so that they always have something exciting to look forward to and can share nice memories of those activities even when life gets ordinary. This allows the couple to avoid the mistake described above.

A prospective spouse has to be informed of the never-ending effort that will be demanded of him throughout the course of a marriage.

It is important for a guy to put his wife first in his life. He may start a conversation with her by inquiring about her day, making some suggestions for potential date locations, and looking for areas of agreement between them. When he treats you with such respect, you know you've met the one you've been looking for all along.

Both on the inside and the outside, he is always looking for new methods to develop himself and become better. Keep in mind that the phrase "making an effort" in a relationship may have a variety of various connotations depending on the person reading it. Because he loves you so deeply, he strives to be successful in all he does so that he can provide a life that is both beautiful and easy for you. He achieves this by working very hard. Even while many women respect the commitment he has for his work, they are concerned that it may come at the price of his passion for them.

recognizes both your positive and your bad characteristics.
There is no way that could make you feel terrible about the shortcomings you have.

Do not put on an act if you believe that is what he is looking for from you. It's possible that you assume that if you're straightforward and truthful with him, your connection to him will only improve. In order to maintain a good relationship, both giving and receiving are required. Because of the way that life works, we should not be surprised when unexpected occurrences take place. It is difficult to look into the future and know that everything will proceed according to plan. In spite of the fact that they would rather be soaking in the rays of the sun, men who are meant to be husbands are trustworthy, helpful, and patient.

Takes into account your input in important as well as minor matters. When interacting with one another, members of a relationship should always see one another as equals, and never as superiors or subordinates. Taking into account your needs and desires demonstrates that he appreciates you and is interested in building a life together with you as opposed to just assimilating you into his own. When we engage into a relationship with another person, even if we are perfectly pleased in our own little worlds, we have to learn to adjust to that other's tastes and interests in order to be happy in the relationship.

Growth-oriented is an approach.
No matter how flawless we may seem to others on the surface, the truth is that we all have our share of imperfections. It is not always simple to uncover a person's shortcomings; yet, a person's greatest strength may often shed light on their greatest vulnerability. You could find that his immaturity has a negative impact on you at times, and the decisions you do will have repercussions for his development (and vice versa). A guy who is sincere about bettering himself would actively seek out methods to improve his moral character. A guy who isn't interested in bettering himself would point the finger at you for his shortcomings and expect you to accept them as acceptable.

Let's pretend for the sake of argument that you're dating a man who doesn't have a lot of empathy simply for fun. It's possible that after you've had a challenging day, rather of trying to comfort you, he gives you good advise instead. His no-nonsense attitude to finding solutions to problems ought to be beneficial to him in business. But it can still be painful when he doesn't get it and gives unsolicited advice on how to solve the problem, or when he loses patience with your hypersensitivity to things that he doesn't give much thought to. Both of these scenarios are examples of situations in which he doesn't get it and offers unsolicited advice.

You need to steer clear of males who put the responsibility for their harsh tone of voice on you, and instead pursue relationships with guys who are willing to work on improving the way they sound. Even though they are unsuccessful at times, a person who is focused on personal improvement will always give it their best effort.

Beliefs and values that are shared

People often fail to recognize this fact, despite the fact that it is patently clear. It is important that you be on the same page with him on everything that really matters if you are going to make him your life partner. Even if you completely disagree with each other's viewpoints, you and he need to have a sufficient amount of respect for each other's positions in order to be able to negotiate a middle ground. It's possible that issues of morals, ethics, where you choose to settle down and whether or not you start a family will come into play here.

You and he become more than simply a relationship when you spend time together. Your combined advantages outweigh those of each of your individual abilities. He does not regard you as a tool to bolster his ego, validate his feelings, or fulfill his demands; rather, he appreciates you as an equal with whom he may develop and become better.

He admires everything about you, from your goals and ideas to what you say and who you surround yourself with, even down to the profession you've chosen for yourself. He does not criticize you or make you feel horrible about yourself or your history in any way.

Maintain constant communication with you. Communicate, despite the fact that sentiments may be harmed or the topic may be sensitive. When you're hanging out with the right person, you can talk about anything without worrying about his response. You may have confidence in his capacity to listen to what you have to say and take into account what you have to say. Each and every one of those connections that has ever existed has been forced to go through its fair share of adversity. There can be moments when one partner does not feel loved, as well as periods of disagreement, misunderstanding, and conflict. These things are inevitable in any committed relationship. The only way to emerge better and stronger on the other side of hardship is to work through it together, communicating in an open and honest manner.

Making preparations to wed you. It can seem to be self-evident, but in point of fact, it's not. If the guy of your dreams has all of these qualities but has no intention of marrying you, then he is not the man of your dreams even if he has all of these attributes. It becomes apparent very early on in most men's lives that their long-term plan is to devote the rest of their life to a single lady. He is certain that he has discovered the one he is meant to be with, and she is as well; yet, it is possible that they may not get engaged right away. It is conceivable that he will tell her, but it is also possible that they will find it out together. Even if they come to the conclusion that now is not the right time to be engaged, he will make it abundantly apparent to her how seriously he takes the relationship. As a result, she will never have to wonder about his dedication to the relationship. If he still plans to live the single, bachelor, party-boy lifestyle, then your aspirations for a wedding are destined to disappointment. If you want to have a long-term relationship with someone, you need be sure that he has the same beliefs as you do. When a guy is prepared for a committed relationship, it is not hard to see the signs. If you find out that is not the case, you should definitely let him know. Men who are thinking about getting married should have a firm grip on this idea. If you find out that he isn't now, rather than finding out later, you will feel a sense of relief.

It is not necessary for a guy to be able to offer in order for a marriage to be happy. Discovering a person who has the faith in you to enable you to take care of yourself while also promising to watch out for your well-being is the most essential step. Finding a spouse who shares your beliefs and passions is one of the most important steps on the path to a good marriage.

one in which one spouse provides emotional support to the other while they are going through a difficult time.

Your commitment to your spouse need to be unwavering if he has the most of the characteristics listed above.

It will be well worth it in the end to stick with this guy despite all of the anticipated mounting tensions and problems that will come your way.

He was the kind of guy who would prioritize you above anything else, no matter what was going on in the world.

If you treat him with the respect due to the man he should marry, he will prove to be all you could have wished for in a partner.

Everyone who is a part of this endeavor has to put in the same level of effort for it to be successful. There is no need to worry about running out since he has more than enough to spare.

CHAPTER THREE

How To be An Ideal Wife?

Hi Guys, Let your affection and warmth for one another shine through. A couple of different races sharing a bed as they sleep. It is essential for a good wife to be able to express her love for her husband in meaningful ways since this is considered to be one of her most significant responsibilities. You should make an effort to find ways to demonstrate your love for him, and explaining your passion for him is an essential piece of guidance that we have for you.

It is common for us to disregard our emotions in favour of placing an excessive amount of importance on the worries, duties, or pressures that we face daily. To the point where we give our loved ones room for interpretation about the depth of our devotion to them when we leave that decision up to them. Take all necessary precautions to prevent this scenario from happening in your married life.

Remember to demonstrate some degree of sympathy. You should make an attempt to be understanding toward your spouse even though it will likely be tough for you to do so. Even though you don't have to be highly tolerant of other people, understanding is a trait that is very useful and highly desirable. Even if you don't have to be understanding of others, you should try to be.

No one of us is faultless, even our spouses, and none of us is perfect. Neither of our spouses is flawless. Although you should make an effort not to be subservient, it is a critical ability that is just as important now as it was 60 years ago to have an awareness of your husband's faults and defects. While you should make an effort not to be subservient, you should also have an understanding of your husband's faults and imperfections.

Above all, do give a careful consideration to the needs of your partner. If you want to be a good wife, you should make an effort to satisfy the criteria of your husband, even if those requirements are different from the standards that a man in the 1950s would have expected from his wife. Despite this, the core idea has not changed in any significant way. It is not necessary to continuously keep a pristine environment, have an excellent temperament, and look their very best in order to effectively cater to his needs.

It does need having empathy for what he may be in need of and searching for ways to either provide it for him or aid him on his road toward achieving his goals. In addition to this, it entails searching for other methods to supply it for him. Make an effort to let your significant other know how much you value and care for them so that they may reciprocate those feelings.

Men rank the ability of their wives to provide them with personal space as the fourth most desirable quality in a partner for their marriage. When it comes to giving your partner their own space, though, finding a happy medium between the two is necessary. If you stay in close proximity to them at all times, there is a chance that you may cause them to feel as if they are being smothered or though they are being suffocated.

Couples that can maintain their individuality more successfully are those who can spend sufficient time away from one another. They could better understand the value of the connection they have with the other person if they are briefly separated from one another.

5. Acknowledge and support the importance of his goals for the cheerful black couple on their way to work

Do you want to have a relationship with another person that is not only good for you but also brings you joy? If you responded "yes," it is crucial to keep in mind that striving towards one's own personal goals is an essential component of all strong relationships. This is something that you should keep in mind since it is essential. If you made an effort to be there for your spouse and supported the goals that they had, it would be helpful for your relationship as a whole. Your partner will appreciate the support.

If you want to assist your husband in accomplishing his goals, you may sometimes need to urge him to exert more effort, or you may just need to be quiet and listen to what he has to say. Either way, your assistance will be much appreciated. It is often vital for you to give them a pep talk in order to raise their spirits and get them inspired again when they are feeling unmotivated. In order to fulfil the role of a spouse who is supportive, one must be willing to engage in a variety of actions of love and consideration alongside their partner while they seek their goals.

Demonstrate a solid ability to argue persuasively. As we very well know that there is no such thing as a partnership without the potential for disagreements of opinion. But the manner in which two different people argue with one another is what actually counts. Finding positive ways to disagree with your spouse is a vital step on the path to being a good wife. There are many constructive ways to do this. Keeping a polite manner amid an argument might teach you valuable lessons about how to become a better wife.

According to the findings of a body of research, the irritability that often surfaces in romantic relationships may be traced straight back to unhealthy patterns of communication between partners. Therefore, even if you and your partner are in an intense dispute, you should exhibit politeness toward one another. You are not compelled to make any compromises about the values that are most important to you; instead, you should treat one another with respect and compassion.

Let's make an effort to live healthy lives together. A youthful couple, both of them are joyful and smiling as they exercise together. Keeping up good relationships with others has the potential to assist both parties involved in leading a healthy way of life. Therefore, if you educate yourself on how to be a good wife, you will be able to convince your husband to lead a healthier lifestyle. This can be accomplished by educating yourself on how to be a good wife. You may want to try working on this jointly at some point.

If you want to be a better wife, you should try to encourage your husband to take better care of his mental and physical health. This will assist you both in the long run. It's possible that you and your partner may benefit from going to therapy together, starting a healthier diet, or joining a gym. All of these things could be beneficial.

Show respect for him at all times, but especially in public situations. Dr Emerson Eggerichs, a communication specialist, is the author of a book titled "Love and Respect Workbook," in which he highlights the value of showing unfettered love and respect for one's partner. Eggerichs thinks that each of these characteristics should be given the same amount of importance. An attitude of respect for another person comprises having sentiments of regard and appreciation for that other person.

Because there is a possibility that insulting your spouse in public might have long-term ramifications, you should be especially careful not to do so anytime you are in a public setting. Your disrespectful conduct toward your spouse in front of other people may make him feel embarrassed, ashamed, enraged, or insecure. This is because it will hurt their pride.

Make sure that your needs are understood. If you are unwilling to help yourself, then no one will be able to aid you. Because this is such a crucial aspect of being a good wife, it is imperative that you make it clear to your partner what it is that you need and what it is that you desire.

The fact that your partner may experience emotions of disconnection from you, perplexity, or irritation is often the result of the fact that it is difficult to ascertain what each individual wants in a relationship. Tell him exactly what it is that you need, and don't allow them the chance to spend an endless amount of time trying to guess what the appropriate answer may be.

Love yourself. Although it would seem to go against common sense, the admonition to love oneself is, in fact, one of the most essential pieces of advice. You will never be able to learn how to be a fantastic wife until you first learn how to love and appreciate the unique person that you are. If you do not do this, you will never be able to learn how to be a wonderful wife.

It is impossible to love another person until one has reached a place where they can love oneself entirely, warts and all. Only then can they love another person. If your connection with yourself is good, then your relationship with your partner will be healthy as well.

Don't let yourself get worked up by the little details of an ebony and white couple who are happy and in love. It is in everyone's best interest to "Let It Go," as Elsa advised; she was right. Every disagreement that might crop up in a marriage is not worth pursuing further. Learn how to let go of the tiny things that grate on your nerves so you can have a better knowledge of how to be a good wife. This is one of the most crucial skills to learn while trying to get a handle on how to be a good wife.

It is unavoidable for there to be a few minor points of contention inside a marriage; nevertheless, if you and your spouse continue to dispute over these issues, your relationship will always be riddled with strife and pressure. Be patient and use your analytical thinking to choose which problems need starting a dispute over while you are deciding which topics warrant starting a fight over.

Confront the issues that are now at hand. Although it can seem that arguments are disruptive and peace can be found in silence, the reality is quite the contrary to this perception. The decision to keep one's mouth shut may at times be seen as an act of denial or avoidance of a topic that may be crucial to the healthy functioning of a relationship.

Research has shown that denying anything is a kind of protective behaviour; yet, this type of conduct may have adverse effects on a relationship that are both short-term and long-term. It's possible that taking care of the issue in a courteous and kind manner would do more than just address the problem; it may also improve the quality of your connection with the other person.

Make it a routine to train yourself to have self-control. Even when things seem to be difficult, you should make an effort to keep your composure since relationships can be pretty hard on one's emotional well-being. However, you should make this effort even when things appear to be going well. The cultivation of self-control is one of the most critical factors contributing to the success of any relationship.

If you give in to your anger and allow it to control you, not only will the problem you're trying to solve become more challenging but so will your husband's feelings about it. Consequently, understanding how to exercise self-control is one of the most essential skills to acquire in order to become a decent wife. It is possible that doing so can help you avoid problems entirely and deal with those that do occur in a responsible and mature way.

Be generous. One of the most valuable pieces of guidance for being a good wife is to show consideration for your partner's feelings and the relationship requirements. This generosity may be seen by the thoughtful words you speak, the caring activities you carry out, and the compassionate manner in which you react to any mistake that your spouse may make.

When you are pleasant to your mate, they will sense sentiments of love and support, and these feelings will come from you. Even though you may disagree with them if you treat them kindness, it will make it easier for your partner to escape the sense of being cornered and singled out. The talk you and your husband are about to have would benefit significantly from beginning with a great mindset on both of your parts. The fact that you are paying attention to what your partner is saying and considering how he is feeling suggests that you care about and consider both of these things. You will have a more profound comprehension of your partner's intentions, characteristics, and feelings if you take the time to listen to them.

Don't forget sex. How about we talk about sexuality? In the majority of marriages, sexual activity is an essential component, and both partners need to put in the effort to ensure that it continues to be exciting for them. Sexual activity is a crucial component. When mastering the skills necessary to be a good wife, it is critical to remember the importance of sex and to make an effort to keep things exciting between the two of you.

Pay attention to your husband and make an attempt to grasp what it is that he expects from his wife in the bedroom by paying attention to what he says and making an effort to understand what he means. In order to avoid either you or your partner from finding a sexual activity to be repetitive or tedious, you can keep an open mind and suggest new things to do.

Anxiety about the welfare of his close family. Marriages aren't always easy, especially during the period of transition that comes after the start of a new family unit. Especially at this time, couples may find themselves in conflict. It may make life easier for both of you if your husband could see that you care about his family. Showing concern for his loved ones might help you both. And demonstrating compassion for his family will bring him a multitude of benefits in the long run.

Your caring manner will show your husband that you have an emotional interest in the things and people who are important to him and that you are worried about them. This will display that you are concerned about the things and people that are important to him. It is likely that it will motivate him to demonstrate care for the individuals who you hold dear to his heart. It's possible that by doing these measures, you'll also be able to fortify the connection that you have with the members of your husband's family.

Take part in one another's favourite activities and hobbies. It may be difficult for the two of you to find activities that you both love doing in your spare time if one of you likes to stay indoors while the other prefers going on walks or different outside activities. But if you want to know how to be a lovely wife, you need to learn how to share a few hobbies with your husband so that the two of you may connect at the same time. If you want to know how to be a lovely wife, you must learn to share a few interests with your husband.

It is not required for you and your partner to have the same passions and activities for your relationship to be successful. On the other hand, the two of you could find a shared interest in venturing into the uncharted areas together and perhaps doing so. Alternately, you may try each other's hobbies and activities to see whether any of them tickle your interest enough to warrant the adoption of one of them as a new activity.

Have fun. Don't forget to have fun! One thing you should bear in mind if you are worried about "how to be a better wife to my husband" is to make things as light and cheerful as much as possible. It has the ability to boost both of your moods and aid in decreasing the quantity of stress that you are feeling; thus, you should try to take advantage of this opportunity. In addition, it could provide your partner with an injection of positive energy that stays with him for the rest of the day.

Be open. Marriage is a commitment that draws two people closer together so that they may spend their lives with one another, and it's called marriage for a reason. A crucial component of this relationship is the understanding reached between the parties that they will continue to approach one another with an open mind and heart. Open communication between partners is associated with the formation of deeper relationships and a greater degree of confidence in the partner's reliability.

In relationships, being open involves letting down your guard and having frank conversations about how you feel with your partner. Relaxing your guard is one strategy that might help you achieve this goal. If you become defensive or put up walls, it is conceivable that your spouse may experience emotions of detachment and irritation. These sentiments may make it difficult for them to communicate with you.

A couple that decides to forgo the usage of any technological gadgets to focus on spending quality time together in the fresh air. You and your partner have to come to an understanding of a particular time or day of the week in which the two of you will put aside your electronic gadgets and give priority to spending time with one another instead. When trying to spend quality time with your significant other, it is crucial to avoid getting distracted by things like mobile phones and other technological gadgets so that you can make the most of your time together.

Put the phone down and attempt to have an open and honest conversation with your partner about what you did all day long by sharing what you did with them. Either you and he may spend time doing something together, like cooking or watching a movie, or you can spend time listening to him talk about the events of his day. You have choices regardless of the outcome.

Make use of the relationships he already has. If you want to learn how to be a good wife, you have to learn how to let your husband have fun with his friends. It is tempting to enjoy your spouse all to yourself, but if you want to learn how to be a good wife, you have to let your husband have fun with his friends. This is a crucial component in the process of becoming a good wife. It will help him become a happier and more satisfied version of who he already is and support him in doing so.

If, on the other hand, you make an effort to prevent him from spending time with his friends, he can get resentful of you, unsatisfied with you, or angry with you if you do so. And most importantly, why not give him a chance to miss you every once in a while by letting him miss you for a bit?

The determination of how much money there is. Money, money, and even more money. You should not place your monetary future in the hands of chance or the complete control of your partner. Instead, take responsibility for it yourself. You should attempt to take matters into your own hands and stick to a budget that is appropriate for the two of you as a couple. This will help ensure that your financial goals are met.

Give him an uplifting compliment. Who here doesn't like hearing nice praise about themselves? Do you? Your husband feels the same way. Spend some time praising your partner for their appearance, how they make you think, and all of the fantastic things they bring to the table regarding your marriage. This will go a long way toward strengthening your bond.

If you see that they are making an effort, it is appropriate to complement the actions that they are making. Compliments may be seen as a kind of affirmation, validation, and incentive to go on behaving constructively in the days and years to come.

Admit mistakes. Always remember to be humble and take full responsibility for your mistakes. To become a good wife, one of the essential things you can do is learn how to take responsibility for your actions and acknowledge your shortcomings. Recognizing that you have done wrong is the most effective approach to lessen the amount of friction inside a marriage, although doing so may be humiliating.

Make sure the Arguments should be there in favour of your being a kind and considerate wife. As we know, Marriages need the involvement of both partners, with each spouse accepting particular obligations for which they are uniquely prepared to care for the household. By educating yourself on the skills essential to be a good wife to your husband, you can help create an environment in your house filled with love and affection for one another.

If your partner notices that you are trying to understand how a woman should treat her man, he may feel compelled to follow in your footsteps and treat you in the same way if he believes that you are setting an excellent example for him. Your hard work and commitment have the potential to motivate your partner, which will finally result in the development of a loving marriage between the two of you.

A married couple runs the danger of growing bored with one another and having a lack of satisfaction in their life together if they take their relationship for granted. This is especially true if they have children together. You can demonstrate to your husband or wife that you value his work by being a kind and considerate wife, or you may choose to carry out the task on your own.

CHAPTER FOUR

Anger Management

Anger management is a term that refers to the use of psychotherapy methods with the purpose of controlling and preventing furious outbursts. Some people have referred to it as "putting one's anger to work," which is essentially what it is. Anger is often the result of frustration or the subject's sense that they are being hindered from attaining something they consider essential. Both of these factors may contribute to the subject's frustration.

Anger that does not dissipate over time is often indicative of an issue with the individual's mental health. According to Ogle, fury is generally associated with anxiety disorders, even though it may be a symptom of various conditions, including those that may make it challenging to manage one's emotions. Nonetheless, Ogle believes anxiety disorders are the most common cause of rage.

If you find that you often feel angry, or if those feelings are causing you issues at home or work, the following are seven suggestions that may assist you in regaining control:

1. Always give some thought before you speak.

One of the most effective strategies is to wait for a moment before responding to anything. Stop what you're doing if your heart is racing and you need to shout at a friend, member of your family, or the person who just drove in front of you in traffic. Take a few deep breaths. Let's count to ten. Try all you can to keep yourself from lashing out and saying or doing anything you'll later come to regret.

2. Once you've regained your composure, explain what it was that disturbed you.

Which of these responses do you think is the most appropriate reaction to what took place? Determine the most profound emotion. Perhaps the fact that your partner didn't assist you in cleaning up the kitchen after you prepared supper makes you feel like you don't matter. Or maybe you feel resentful because your kid took your vehicle and returned it to you with the petrol tank almost completely depleted - for the second time. Address the event and individual plainly and directly, using an "I" statement. For instance, you may say, "I'm unhappy because you left me without enough petrol to go to work", or "I dislike it when I labour to prepare a dinner, and you don't help clean up afterwards." These are examples of things that could make someone upset.

3. To relieve stress, make lighthearted jokes.

Bringing some humour into the situation might help relieve tension. Make light of the situation that has you worked up by using comedy to get you through it. You should make fun of yourself for having such unrealistic ideas about how things should happen. Laugh at your own mistakes, but stay away from sarcasm. It often seeks to harm others to make a point about how the speaker feels about themselves. Also, avoid acting in a passive-aggressive manner.

4. Call a break and regroup.

Timeouts aren't only for youngsters. Being self-aware of your energy level is crucial to take care of your needs and being the best you can be. Take some time off for yourself during the parts of the day that are often the most stressful. You could feel more prepared to manage what's coming up without being upset or furious if you take a few minutes to have some peace.

5. Get exercise.

Getting some exercise may help relieve stress, which can be a contributing factor to irritability. It is common practice to recommend physical activity to lift one's mood. Endorphins are natural mood boosters and stress relievers, and they are created in the body as a response to physical effort. If you feel your anger rising, take a quick walk, run, or engage in any other fun physical activity for a while. This will help you calm down.

6. Develop your ability to relax via practice.

Providing calming input to any of your six senses, or all of them may help you feel more at ease. You can relax by doing exercises that involve deep breathing, getting a warm drink, smelling some pleasant scents, going outside and feeling the crisp air, stretching your muscles, imagining a relaxing scene, listening to relaxing music, or repeating a word or phrase that soothes you, such as "Take it easy." Yoga and meditation are two more helpful practices that might assist you in maintaining your composure. It is much simpler to manage the obstacles that life places in front of you if you take good care of yourself first.

7. Don't harbour a grudge.

The ability to forgive others is a powerful weapon. Keeping a grudge against someone else in the hopes that they would feel your anguish or make up for their mistake only affects you in the long run. If you allow anger and other bad sentiments to drown out happy sensations, you risk becoming consumed by your feelings of resentment or a sense that something unfair has been done to you. However, if you can forgive the person who wronged you (that is if you cancel the debt that is due to you), you can let go of the burden and are no longer burdened by the need for "payback."

Everyone, at specific points in their lives, has the problem of needing to master the art of anger management. If making adjustments such as these does not help you get better control of your anger, you should seek the assistance of a mental health professional. If your rage appears out of control, leads you to do things you later regret, or causes you or people around you to injure others, you should get therapy for anger problems.

Although there is no known treatment for anger, it is possible to regulate both the intensity of your feelings and their effect on you. It is possible to obtain helpful therapeutic methods for anger management, which might aid you in becoming less reactive. These solutions could be found in a variety of settings. You may even teach yourself to be more patient in the face of other people and events beyond your control by practising this trait often. It is possible to lessen the effect of being angry on your life by using strategies that might help you manage your anger. There is nothing you can do to get rid of anger since it is a normal emotion and feeling everyone experiences. On the other hand, you may get the abilities required to regulate it appropriately.

The feeling of fury has the potential to be very powerful. When you find yourself in a circumstance that leads you to feel sad, hurt, angry, or disappointed, it is a normal and healthy reaction that you have. It is also a response that you have. It might result from something that occurs to you, something that someone else said or did, or something that you remember. All of these things could be factors. It's possible that any or all of these factors are at fault. It all comes down to how you deal with your anger; it may either help or hurt you in the long run. It would be advantageous if you could react to the situation without endangering anybody else. It may be beneficial when we need to defend ourselves, and it may encourage you to change how things are currently being done. However, it also can convince you to behave in ways you really ought not to do.

Keeping your wrath bottled up within might lead to you engaging in passive-aggressive actions such as "getting back" at other people without expressing why you are doing so or being critical and rude toward them. If you can understand these sensations and tell them appropriately, you will be better equipped to deal with unexpected situations, find solutions to difficulties, and maintain meaningful relationships. If you can understand these sensations and express them appropriately, you will be able to represent them appropriately.

Anger is a symptom that is related with a number of other mental health difficulties, despite the fact that anger is not a problem in and of itself it is associated with a number of other mental health disorders.

CHAPTER FIVE

MISTAKES BY HUSBAND

It is quite probable that a profound and pervasive lack of satisfaction is at the bottom of every unhappy marriage. A perception that there is a lack of essential components for a satisfactory relationship, such as love, affection, trust, and respect, among other things. By nature, a woman is more linked to her emotions.

The following is a list of some of the most typical justifications that spouses provide for ending their marriages:

- *Overly Dominant*
-

Unappreciative

- *Insufficiently complimentary*

- *Lacking an apology*

Instead, what they need to be doing is:

1. Stay away a little

2. Don't argue at all.

3. Never speak about prior events

The significance of this link likely varied depending on which side you asked. Because of this, the mere fact that you decide to end the affair does not guarantee that the other person will respect your choice or even that you will. The "Break-up, Make-up" cycle is a regular occurrence throughout an affair. But you won't be able to put your marriage back together unless you take a stance and completely cut off communication with your spouse. Nevertheless, you should not be naïve; the next effort or impulse to connect will likely present itself. If you deny an imminent reality, you will make yourself more susceptible to relapse. So, prepare yourself for having to wholly and firmly deny communication.

If you want to bring healing to your marriage after a betrayal, you can't continue living your life as usual and expect it to work. Your normal behaviour is what got you into this situation. It is necessary to make adjustments to demonstrate to your partner that you are accepting responsibility for the issue and taking preventative measures to ensure that it will not recur. There are probably problems in every marriage, but the present moment is not the right time to address such issues. First things first, you need to demonstrate that you are committed to the relationship and that it is stable. Then, after the rift in the connection has been patched up, you may go on to address the other problems. Early on, the unfaithful spouse must learn to enjoy the focus on their own life before any concerns inside the betrayed spouse can be explored. Your actions are the only foundation a spouse who has been harmed may use to start healing. If you are persistent and do what you say, then your companion might trust you again with time. But if you fail to follow through with what you say, it will strengthen your mate's scepticism. You must express what you mean and mean what you say. Do not fall into the trap of giving your partner what you believe she or he wants to hear but failing to follow through on what you promised. You will be a lot better off if you're realistic and then do what you say, even if what you say (and then do) is not as spectacular as you or your companion had hoped.

CHAPTER SIX

MISTAKES BY WIFE

Many people don't like it when you try to change their way of life against their will, and one of those people is you. They get the impression that you are holding up their shortcomings in front of them, which may be discouraging and drive down morale. This is one of the mistakes women make while interacting with guys, and it is a mistake uniquely associated with the male gender.

One of the most powerful methods for giving constructive criticism to another person is to do it compassionately. The vast majority of the time, it is more productive to provide constructive feedback than negative criticism. It is disrespectful to hastily judge another person based on the shortcomings they may have. You should let them know that you are aware of what they are doing and encourage them to enhance their performance while also letting them know that you are aware of what they are doing.

In addition, if you want your partner to change the things they do or the way they go about their lives, you can have a difficult time convincing them to do so since they are used to the way they live. As a consequence of this, the strategy that will prove to be the most fruitful is to engage in conversation with them while attempting to have an open mind. At some time, you and your spouse will figure out how to prevent hurting one another by finding a middle ground that strikes a balance between the two extremes.

When two people are in a romantic relationship, it is the responsibility of both individuals to take whatever steps are necessary to ensure that the other person is content with the connection.

To maintain a healthy marriage, both you and your spouse need to express gratitude and appreciation for one another on a regular basis. Recognize the importance of what your partner has done for you and make it a top priority to return the favour as quickly as you can.

There are some women who are oblivious to the amount of effort that went into the favour that they get, and as a consequence, they are ungrateful for the assistance they receive. Your partner will be more encouraged to put in further effort if you demonstrate that you acknowledge and appreciate their efforts, regardless of how huge or small they may be. This is true whether the steps are large or small.

Being jealous of the other individuals in your partner's life with whom they have connections. It is usual for a person who is in love with their partner to experience some amount of jealousy toward other individuals, but when this emotion becomes excessive, it may be detrimental to the relationship. Jealousy is natural for someone who is in love with their partner. Women often make the mistake of thinking that they should have free access to their partner's life and that there should be no place for other people in the relationship. This is one of the most prevalent dating mistakes that women make.

On the other hand, this is a false assumption because before you met your spouse, they already had other aspects of their lives in which different people, such as friends, acquaintances, colleagues, and the like, played a part. Therefore, it would not be a terrible thing at all if your spouse is very close to some of them, and you do not need to allow it to interfere with your relationship in any way. You do not need to enable it to interfere with your relationship.

If you feel that your partner is giving you a little more attention than is customary, you should discuss it with them and express your displeasure in a level-headed and reasonable way. To avoid giving your partner the appearance that you are possessive and too jealous of them, the two of you need to create an environment in which you may feel secure and at ease in your relationship.

Providing your spouse with an inadequate amount of personal space. Before you and your partner decided to have a family together, each of you was a unique individual with your responsibilities. The same is true of your partner before the two of you chose to start a family together. Because doing so is harmful to both of you, it is not in either of your best interests to restrict the scope of your relationship to just the two of you as a couple.

Even if your significant other is the essential thing in your life, you don't need to be possessive of them since they will ultimately want some time to themselves at some point. Even if they are the essential thing in your life, you should not be possessive of them.

Give your spouse a chance to have fun with their friends, acquaintances, and other people in their social circle, and spend time participating in activities that bring them happiness. You are more than welcome to join them occasionally; yet, there will be other occasions when you should leave them space to be alone. After entering into a committed relationship or being married, some women begin to get the misconception that their partner will remain with them for the rest of their lives. As a result of the belief that this is true, they make minimal effort to ensure that their spouses continue to find them attractive. During the time you spend at home with your significant other, it won't hurt to demonstrate to them that you still have it in you to dress in a sexually suggestive way. It is necessary to make this an ongoing component of your routine; it is essential to preserve a pleasant scent and a clean look at all times. Moreover, it is necessary to clean up after yourself. You should also anticipate a rise in the self-assurance that comes along with this change as a result of the change, as mentioned earlier.

Participating in a large number of acts of hostile indifference. Passive aggressiveness may be shown by actions such as being silent in the face of unpleasant emotions such as rage or despair. Another form of passive aggression is avoiding eye contact. Certain women have this temperament, which may be rather difficult for the males in relationships with such ladies.

When your significant other notices that you are not in a good mood, it is advisable to be upfront and honest with them about what is going on rather than keeping them in the dark about what is happening. The truth is that coping with passive hostility requires significant energy. The other spouse may get worn out due to the situation and decide to ignore you the next time they see you are irritated.

Just because your spouse did something that made you uncomfortable does not mean you have to respond with passive hate against them. You should avoid being dramatic about it and be open to openly discussing it with them and eager to do so.

Including or incorporating other individuals into your own life or relationship. It is natural for a relationship to have friction now and then, and the majority of the time, the most productive way to address these issues is for the two of you to sit down and hash things out on your own. You also can seek advice from a counsellor, which you should do if you find yourself in a situation in which you and your spouse are obliged to answer to the same individual. Aside from these particular circumstances, you are not advised to let any other third party get involved in the problem that is occurring inside your relationship. If you get terrible advice, it may hurt your relationship. This is likely to happen in the great majority of situations.

In addition, whomever you seek advice from will likely take your side rather than remain neutral in the circumstance if they are the ones from whom you seek advice. The successful settlement of internal conflicts gives your partner the impression that you hold them in high esteem, which enhances the possibility that they will work with you the next time you want their assistance.

Having a perpetually negative outlook on life. Being a pessimist is one of the things you need to avoid doing if you don't want to mess up in your romantic relationships. If you don't want to mess up in your romantic relationships, you must stay clear of being a pessimist. You don't need to disregard any thoughts or recommendations your partner provides just because you have concluded that you are correct and have proven this to yourself. It is difficult for one person to always be in the wrong in a relationship since the connection's health depends on the combined efforts of both parties.

There are more fruitful ways to handle the matter than to be harsh about it, even if you think that your partner is the one who is in the wrong in this argument. When your spouse makes a suggestion, you should try to resist being judgmental of them and complaining about them.

Your significant other does not seem to have an adequate incentive in you to maintain the connection they now have with you. People like being inspired, especially by those they care about the most since it encourages them to push themselves to achieve even greater success. You have to lead a life that will make your spouse want to appreciate you and drive them to want to respect you. You have to achieve this by leading a life that will make them want to enjoy you. If you remain in your comfort zone while your partner focuses on bettering themselves, your partner may get aggravated with you at some point in the future.

Therefore, while your spouse strives to improve their life, you should also focus on improving your own. This will allow you to support your spouse in their endeavours better. When two people are in a committed relationship, it is reasonable to anticipate that they will grow as individuals and as emotional beings in tandem with one another. This goal may be attained by concentrating on and improving various aspects of one's life.

Evaluate your relationship's strength by comparing it to that of other people. It is necessary to emphasize that engaging in comparative analysis impedes the growth of intimacy and affection in a romantic connection. One of the mistakes a woman makes when she does not put a high value on her relationship is that she compares her spouse to other people in her life, particularly other men. It's just a fact of life that you probably won't discover a partner with every quality you seek, and that's OK with us. It is not a sound strategy to begin contrasting them with other people in the community in the expectation that this would inspire them to alter their behaviour. If you do this, your partner may start behaving in a way that is geared toward giving you what you want.

In the long run, your link will surely give you an erroneous impression of proximity to the other person. Always remember why you chose your partner in the first place, and under no circumstances should you ever suggest that they copy what you do because of you. Keep in mind why you chose your partner in the first place.

CHAPTER SEVEN

How to Win Your Wife?

Your first order of business should be to listen carefully to what your wife has to say. It was not my intention to imply that you should carry out every one of her directives, and I apologize for any confusion this may have caused. However, if you want to win your wife's affection, you must pay attention to the things going on inside her mind. Acknowledge the significance the importance of her views and feelings. Believe it or not, women are more aware of the pressures on their relationships and often advise on how these partnerships may be better. This is something that men tend to be less aware of. Therefore, taking the time to listen to your wife with an open mind might be of aid to you in determining the cause of the disagreement between the two of you. Put aside your pride and fight the need to protect yourself at any cost. It is not necessary. You should focus on actively listening to her, asking for her opinion, and being forthright about your discoveries. You should continue doing this once a week or maybe even once a month; the more often you do it, the

simpler it will be for your wife to communicate her thoughts and desires.

A guy must make sure that his wife is aware of everything that is going on in his thoughts and heart. Share your feelings. You need to have the mental fortitude to show her that you cannot stand up for yourself and are susceptible to her manipulation. It is difficult for men to discuss with their wives in the same fashion they would with their male friends. Guys cannot converse with their wives in the same manner that they would with other men. When it comes to male communication partners, women prefer guys who exhibit characteristics such as empathy, friendliness, openness, and honesty. Your wife has a pathological need to know all there is to know about you and the way you spend your time. Therefore, sharing everything is the most effective way to show her that you value and include her. This will also show her that you appreciate her. They are interested in whatever you say, so tell them about your day and even the most upsetting memories you have from your childhood.

Give Them a Helping Hand In today's contemporary culture, where most married couples have both the husband and the woman working, many elements add to stress. One of these issues is the fact that the majority of married couples have children. Wives often have obligations at home in addition to the commitments they have to their work. What kind of services do you provide? No matter what you come up with, as long as it assists her in carrying less weight, it will be acceptable. You may assist her by folding her clothes, filling her gas tank, making supper, cleaning the house, or helping the children with schoolwork. Even while it may not take up a significant amount of your time, providing her with help might be something that significantly influences her day. Make her feel you are there for her and that you are standing by her side by giving the appearance that you are there for her.

Believe me when I say that your wife wants to know how you feel about her and wants you to show her that you appreciate her. She also wants you to show her that you enjoy the fact that she is your wife. Whether or not they are sufficient is always on the minds of women. Compliments that come out of the blue are often the ones that are given with the greatest sincerity. When you think lovely things about your wife, you shouldn't keep such ideas to yourself; share them with others instead. Appreciate everything she has done for you, even the little things like minding your children or being there for you. She has gone above and beyond for you. She deserves your thanks. A straightforward demonstration of appreciation for her might enhance her day and give her the sense that you value her contribution. Compliment her on how well she has dressed or anything else you find appealing about her. She'll appreciate hearing it. Compliments are something that women eagerly anticipate hearing, and when they do, it may urge them to put more effort into the connection that they have with the person who has complimented them.

In the same way that when you desire something, you pay attention to the care that it requires, whether it be your home or your vehicle, you should educate her about the world. The institution of marriage does not provide an exception to this norm. If you want your relationship to be successful, you will need to put in the work to rebuild the empathy and commitment that once existed between the two of you. You should attempt to convey to her the sense that she is a unique individual who is cherished, cared for, and respected. You need to get her to reevaluate how she feels about you and to start falling in love with you all over again. You should do all in your power to attract her, such as sending her flowers or writing her poetry. She could just give in to your charms. Express to her how much you care about her and how far you are willing to go to make things right between the two of you. Tell her how much you love her. The solution to the question of what it takes to win a woman's affection may be found right here. Give her the idea that she is unique in order for her to understand that you do not take the connection for granted, which is something that you should not do regardless of the circumstances. If you haven't previously shown her how much you appreciate all she's done for you over the last few months, now could be the perfect opportunity to do so if you haven't already done so in the past. It is not necessary for it to be an expensive present; rather, you should make an effort to locate anything uncomplicated that will make her day more enjoyable. Believe me when I say that sending someone a thoughtful note or offering appreciation at the appropriate moment may go a very long way.

CHAPTER EIGHT

How to Win Your Husband?

Hey extraordinary ladies, Make sure he has enough space to breathe. Your first response would probably be to beg and plead with your spouse to put more effort into the relationship. This is a perfectly reasonable first step to take. If he has already left, doing that is probably not the wisest line of action since he has already left.

Give the person to whom you have married some space and time so that he may sort through his emotions and work through the issues. Likely, obtaining clarification with the aid of a professional will not be feasible at this time, even though this should be done as soon as possible. You show that you respect his right to have his feelings even though you have a different view when you give him space. This is the case even when you see things differently than he does. If you continue to pressure him, there is a bigger chance that he may back down and stop participating in the dispute.

Suppose you are a husband whose wife has "unilaterally" decided that she wants to divorce. She is unwilling to get marriage help from a professional or seek marriage counselling. In that case, you will have to learn ways to stop the divorce and win her back before you can do anything about it. If she is unwilling to get marriage help from a professional or seek marriage counselling, you will have to learn ways on your own to stop the divorce and win her back.

Probably, your wife never mentioned to you in any way that she was thinking about divorcing you, which is why the news probably came as a total shock to you.

It is not uncommon for women to experience feelings of being overwhelmed and physically "tapped out" when it comes to the children, the cooking, the cleaning, and all of the caretaking duties that they fulfil in all their interactions with their close family members. This is especially common when it comes to caring for children.

When your wife eventually stopped being a nuisance and fell into a hush, that was the indication for her to start making plans for the divorce. She had been waiting for this moment for a long time. And you were oblivious that she was even experiencing negative emotions.

Also, Recognize that you are accountable for the role you play. Changing yourself is the only option when dealing with a partner who is resistant to change. Because of this, you are obligated to accept responsibility for your role in the relationship breakdown. Both of you are to blame for how your relationship has progressed to where it is now and how it got to this point. Even if you did nothing but let it travel on autopilot, the effects of entropy would still take place, and the gap would continue to grow if you did not actively expend energy.

Find out what you were doing that was adding to the environment that made your partner want to pull away from the relationship and address those issues. Bring to your notice the activities you may have been engaging in more often to keep your relationships alive. As you have a deeper comprehension of your role in the partnership, you will be able to initiate more beneficial alterations to the connection. If your spouse observes a change in you, they may respond similarly.

Make sure you Stop nagging. Nagging is a terrible habit that might make a partner want to break up with you. Stop doing it immediately if you are currently engaging in this behaviour. It is not surprising that you would like to bother them since you feel threatened by them.

After all, your spouse does not heed the advice you provide them to carry out the tasks you specify. Investigate the method in which you are asking the things you need, and educate yourself on how to ask more productively. Your spouse will want nothing more than to get away from you if you continue to annoy and prod them if you behave in this manner.

Even if your wife has wholly given up on you, you will still need to put in EXTRA EFFORT to evolve into a man who is more attentive and in touch with his spouse. This is the only way you can become the man she can spend the rest of her life with. Make friends with her. She's great. Be there for her while she is sick, and help her no matter what, even if she has chosen another man over you. She may need you more than anybody else.

We have heard the story of a man who made it his goal to make friends with his wife, even going so far as to help her move out of the house and into a new living arrangement with another man! Extreme conditions, but in the end, the woman decided to return to her husband because she knew she could speak to him about anything, and she understood that their connection would last regardless of the circumstances.

Men, There should be no criticism, nagging, excessive calling, begging, pleading, buying gifts, requesting the support of her family members or friends, following her about, or acting as though you need anything. It is almost as if you are required to entirely disassociate yourself from your identity to be a genuine friend to her. This demands you to be empathic toward her without attempting to repair the problem or provide advice and to engage in continuous acts of selflessness toward her that are free from judgment. In addition, you must have a positive attitude and a robust demeanour, acting as if you do not have any concerns and will be successful in life regardless of the challenges presented to you.

Practice Zero negativity. Not only is persistent nagging harmful to relationships, but so is criticism in even its most basic form. Criticizing, blaming, or humiliating our spouse may come naturally, yet, such behaviour may be highly off-putting to the other person in the relationship since it goes against their instincts. Nobody enjoys being the target of another person's lousy energy because it puts them in a situation they would rather avoid. If you are dissatisfied with anything, you must figure out how to talk about it in a manner that conveys your emotions without making the other person feel bad about themselves.

Acquiring the ability to communicate your ideas in such a manner is a talent that should not be overlooked. This is risky and will taint the connection if this does not alter. Getting rid of the problematic features of your relationship is one way to show your spouse that things have the potential to improve.

Remember to Love in all its many forms and expressions. Figure out how to love your spouse in a way that will allow her to experience that love in the manner in which she expects to be loved. Even if you may have the idea that you have shown love to your girlfriend throughout the years, most of your efforts will have been in vain if you cannot communicate properly with her. Suppose she shares her love through words of affirmation, but you demonstrate your love for her through acts of service, such as making her coffee in the morning, washing the dishes, or putting the children to bed.

In that case, your hard work may not necessarily be interpreted as love unless you also express your love and appreciation for her through words. For example, if her love language is acts of service, such as making her coffee in the morning, washing the dishes, or putting the children to bed, then her love language is words. Even though this is not how you would typically show your love for her, you should start loving her in the way that she demands, even if this is not how you would typically showcase your affection for her. If you want your wife back, you should be doing this as it will give her the idea that you care about her a great deal. If you do this, she will think that you care about her a lot.

Take notice when your spouse engages in constructive behaviour. It is not hard at all to determine whether or not your spouse is participating in conduct that is not proper. It is much harder to catch him doing something right than it used to be. Keep an eye out for that kind act or thoughtful phrase, and when you come across it, make it a point to let him know how much you appreciate it. Instead of starting to believe that there is nothing he can do in this relationship to improve it to the point where he has given up, he will begin to think that the other person is acknowledging and appreciating all of the efforts he is making. This will prevent him from giving up on the relationship altogether. If his actions are recognized and appreciated, it may be possible to get rid of the sentiments of bitterness and impotence, and it may also be possible to restore optimism.

Acclimate your ears to the habit of paying to listen. If your partner has become emotionally distant from the relationship, she will likely ask herself, "Why to bother?" If one partner feels that the other is ignoring or failing to understand them, it may seem as if there is no use in continuing to be in a relationship with that other person. Conversations are suppressed, feelings are smothered, and anger and wrath begin to rise to the surface as a result. When you learn to listen to your spouse by focusing on her and not responding or reacting to what she says, she will finally understand that you care more about what she has to say than what you have to say. This can be accomplished by listening to your spouse, focusing on her, and not responding or reacting to what she says. This may be done by cultivating the skill of attentive listening to one's partner by concentrating one's attention on the partner in question without responding or reacting to anything the partner says. She can tell what's on her mind without worrying about being contradicted or having her point of view discredited.

At long last, she has the impression that her thoughts and feelings are being considered. It is a massive step in differentiating yourself from your spouse and acknowledging your partner's one-of-a-kind qualities if you can learn how to listen to them even when you disagree with what they say. Suppose your spouse gets the impression that you genuinely appreciate who she is. In that case, she will be more likely to want to be in a relationship with you when it is of this type, and she will be more likely to be in a relationship with you when it is of this kind.

Have compassion. It may be difficult to cohabit with a spouse who is emotionally distant or contemplating ending the relationship if one of these conditions exists. You want him to stay, but at the same time, it's tough for you to deal with the anguish of the damage being done to your feelings due to his presence. Because of this, you will often feel pressured to behave in a way that is counterproductive to accomplishing the objectives you have set for yourself. You can alter the trajectory of this relationship simply by demonstrating compassion to your spouse. Your feelings are essential, but you should also remember that your spouse has their own experiences to draw on. There is no right or wrong answer to this question. Arouse compassion inside your heart as you envision your spouse's agony or try to comprehend what may be motivating his behaviours. This will help you be more understanding and compassionate toward your relationship. Imagine a small child who wants nothing more than to be loved and made feel like they are essential. A little boy with an unblemished reputation may be tucked away below his rough, adult persona.

Put yourself in his position and make an effort to comprehend the reasons that underlie his choices. This will encourage you to replace judgment with curiosity, which will help you change how you perceive him and make it easier for you to get along with him.

Put a halt to this public display of contempt. When you feel entirely alone in your relationship, it is tempting to bring in other people, mainly if your spouse is not interested in partnering with you on a project. This is especially true when you are feeling utterly alone in your relationship.

This is particularly true if your partner is not interested in cooperating with you on a project. Be cautious because the more individuals become involved, the more disorder there will be. This usually nearly has the opposite effect of what you want and tends to push your spouse even more away from you. You may wish to have a close friend assist you through this situation; however, involving his family members or calling his friends to persuade him to get into a marriage contract is not always the best decision. You may wish to have a close friend assist you through this situation. You should contact the help you need, but try to keep the issue from becoming a three-ring circus.

It is a very lonely, terrifying, and dreadful experience to live with a spouse who is unwilling to work on the relationship or even threatens to terminate the marriage. Living with a partner reluctant to work on the relationship is a terrible experience. It is not hard to lose trust in something or someone when it seems that it will be challenging to change another individual's viewpoint. Surprisingly, there is still a significant amount that you can do on your end to provide your connection with an additional chance to succeed.

CHAPTER NINE

Home Management

It is the art of managing the home, home affairs and house management activities.

Managing your house is simply ensuring that everything in it continues to function normally. This encompasses everything from going food shopping and preparing meals to clean and putting things away in their proper places.

And although it may not seem like the most glamorous activity, it is crucial to ensuring that your home is a happy and healthy place for your family. You are looking for home management advice that is straightforward and uncomplicated to use in your day-to-day activities.

The act of ensuring that everything in your home continues to work correctly is all that is required to manage your home effectively. This includes everything from going grocery shopping and cooking meals to cleaning and putting things back in their appropriate locations. It also includes putting things away.

There should not be anybody in a home that is being managed well who feels as if they are being overloaded by the day-to-day tasks. Instead, everyone should be aware that they are making a contribution to the machine's efficient running, and as a result, they should feel a sense of self-assurance and competency.

The management of the family becomes almost automatic when everyone gives what they are able to and accomplishes their fair part of the work. It is not about doing everything perfectly; rather, it is about figuring out what works for you, your family, and all of you together as a unit.

And although while it may not seem to be the most exciting thing to do, it is really necessary in order to make sure that your house is a pleasant and healthy place for your family to spend their time. You are seeking for home management advice that is easy to understand and use in your day-to-day activities, and you want it to be as simple as possible. This includes anything from keeping one's finances organized and paying one's bills to maintaining a clean house and preparing one's own meals for oneself and their family.

Keeping order and cleanliness in your own home comes with a number of benefits that should not be overlooked. To give you just one example, it may save you from having to spend money on costly repairs in the future.

When performed on a regular basis, upkeep and maintenance have the potential to assist in the early discovery of potential problems, allowing for resolution of these issues before they may cause substantial damage. After you have a general idea of what needs to be cleaned, create a cleaning plan and try your best to stick to it as much as possible. In addition to the regular cleaning that has to be done, you should also make sure not to forget about important maintenance tasks such as testing the smoke alarms and changing the air filters. To keep your house in excellent shape, you will need to pay attention to a lot of things, including those that were just mentioned.

In addition to this, a home that is well-managed is often warmer and more inviting than a home that is not kept in an adequate manner. The most efficient administration of a home should make life easier and less stressful for all members of the household by cutting down on the amount of labor that must be done. When we pay attention to and take care of the insignificant aspects of a task, we free up more time in our schedules and increase the amount of energy we have available to put our focus on the aspects of our work that are most important to us. The following are some ideas that may be of use to you in the process of developing an efficient home management system:

Maintain a level of simplicity. Do not set yourself the task of tracking each and every thing in your home as a primary priority. Focus your focus on the things that are most important to you and the people who are important to you in your life.

Be consistent. The success of every system is directly proportional to how well it maintains its consistency. You won't go very far with this if all you do is make a record of your cleaning regimen from time to time. Check that your weekly plan includes time for you to update your system and make sure that you do this.

Get everyone involved. Participation from all members of the family is necessary for a home management system to be successful and is thus required for its implementation. Make sure that everyone is aware of how the system works and where they can get the information that they are looking for.

Keep an open mind. As a result of this, you must ensure that you are constantly prepared to make any required modifications to your system. If you attempt something and it doesn't go the way you thought it would, you shouldn't be afraid to try something different since there are plenty of other options.

CHAPTER TEN

Foolish Expectations

I rely on you to be a dependable working partner, and if I want to take a break for roughly a month between jobs, I should be permitted to do so without feeling like it is a burden on you or anybody else. This is because I count on you to be a reliable working partner. And this is true for you, my sweetheart, so don't forget that.

I want to share my life with someone who has lived an entire life and learned a lot of valuable lessons along the way, and I hope that person will be my partner. I don't want to be with someone who constantly gives me the answer yes. I am interested in engaging in constructive debates. I want there to be someone in my life who I can model myself after and look up to. I want you to put up some effort and accept responsibility for some facets of your life. I am going to have complete confidence in the decisions that you come to. I promise!

When it comes to helping out around the house with things like cooking, cleaning, and other activities, if you are not familiar with them already, I want you to learn them with me if possible. We may explore various culinary traditions and styles by working together.

Virgin? Great! Not a virgin? Still having no problems! On the other hand, I think it's best if you don't spend too much time thinking about your ex-significant other. And if you want to talk about him, you should tell me how much better off I am than he was and how awful he was - -if you want to talk about him.

I do not want you to give me money, not even one cent. I want our relationship to begin from scratch as we build our future with you. If difficulty presents itself, I want every one of us to make the necessary efforts to find a solution. If I earn enough money, you should still help me out when I'm in need, even if it means we won't have to endure hardships together.

The fact that I want to be married to you should indicate that I think you are desirable and enticing. I hope that even after you've tied the knot, you'll still have the same allure that you had before. We can go to the gym or do yoga together if you'd like. But please don't go about slacking off and fooling yourself into believing that just because you're married, now you don't have to worry about trying to make a good impression on me with how your body looks anymore.

After a certain period, I intend to go back to live with my parents. They are older individuals who don't create any problems, as far as I can see, and I can attest to that. They will treat you like their own daughter due to the challenges their daughter has had in her married life, so you can expect them to do this. Remarkably, my biological father. I only ask that you show them respect when they are older since it is something they have earned. If there is a problem, I am obligated to address it; you are not responsible. You need not be worried; you won't be responsible for their feeding or care in any way. I will!

I'm on the hunt for a friend who doesn't partake in the following vices: smoking, drinking alcohol, or eating meat. If you choose to drink alcohol occasionally, I won't hold it against you in any way. I have long since given up trying anything new, but if you want to spice up some of our nights, we could try something new together, like sharing some wine and cheese.

CHAPTER ELEVEN

HAPPINESS MANTRAS

Always remember to have a productive and cheerful attitude. There is a possibility that you may take joy in your marriage if you make the conscious decision to concentrate on the favourable features of your connection. The upbeat manner of one's spouse can motivate the partner's optimistic behaviour, which, in turn, may make you and the partnership happier.

If this is not the case, you should attempt to learn what worries your spouse and work toward addressing those worries. If this is the case, you should not make this effort.

Talk Often, Friends! Maintain open channels of communication with one another and make an effort to concentrate more on listening.

It is essential to avoid avoiding communication with the people who are important to you since doing so might put a strain on the connections you have. Try talking to yourself about the difficulties you're going through rather than telling other people about them.

Don't make every discussion about how you feel, what you want, or what you need. Instead, focus on the other person and what they have to say. Learn the art of attentively listening to the things that are important to your partner and communicating openly and honestly with them.

When you feel your spouse is the source of your misery or sadness, it is important to respond appropriately and take the necessary steps. It is best to steer clear of talks that will only serve to make things more complicated.

It is essential to steer clear of the behaviour known as stonewalling, which happens when one spouse refuses to speak with the other, keeps silent, ignores them, or even abandons them for some time.

Stonewalling is a typical cause of anger and irritation, and both of these emotions may make current problems in marriage much more difficult to deal with.

Both of the Competing Parties Should Be Considered Equal The institution of marriage ought to be seen as that of a partnership, one in which the two parties involved are to be accorded the status of equals. Therefore, if you want to have a happy marriage, you must refrain from thinking of yourself as more important than your partner regularly does. A mindset like that might be detrimental to the health of your relationship.

Remember to Be Understanding. Another feature essential to a marriage or committed partnership is the ability to understand one another rather than concentrating on how well the other person in the relationship understands one another.

Do Try to put yourself in the other person's shoes and picture what it would be like. Attempt to understand what it is that your spouse or partner is going through or experiencing by trying to put yourself in their shoes. This may be what drives him or her to behave the way they do.

It is essential to make an effort to connect with those sentiments if you want to have a happy married life. If you want to be satisfied in your marriage, you should.

An Examination of the Differences Between Expectations and Regrets
If your expectations aren't met, you incur the danger of unhappiness, which may commonly lead to

resentment in a marriage or other committed connection. If your expectations aren't satisfied, you also risk being let down.

If they are not resolved or discussed, these grudges can lead to the breakup of a marriage or other significant relationship if they are not handled.

Although lowering your expectations might indeed be helpful, doing so would equal suffocating your desires, which is not a realistic option. Having lower expectations can be beneficial. It is good to live in the present with fewer expectations of the future and to find happiness in the moments that are occurring right now. Living in the now may assist with this.

Discover where the solutions are.
If you and your partner are going through difficult times in your marriage, which is not unusual, then it will take some time for the key difficulties to be resolved. And if things go out of hand, you will need the support of an outside party or the direction of a trained expert.

Even though I have my fair share of highs and lows, I prioritise working through them as swiftly as possible. You have to keep working on it because there will be moments when it takes longer for your spouse to realize something, and there will also be instances when it takes longer to resolve an issue; nonetheless, you should not give up.

Remember that you need to get answers to your queries as quickly as possible if there is a temper tantrum or a conflict.

Find out where the problem stems from and investigate possible solutions to it to prevent it from occurring again in the near or distant future. It is best to put the past in its proper place, to forgive and forget, and to go on to a more joyful existence as a married couple.

Have Fun and Frolic: Laugh it up and enjoy one other's company as you spend quality time together. To find happiness, having a childlike attitude is essential, playing as you did when you were younger, and trying to keep things interesting in your marriage.

Do not place excessive importance on what you believe about yourself. It is a waste of time to get into verbal altercations with other people since life is made up of fleeting moments that are precious in and of themselves.

Be Responsible and Understanding: You are the only one who can guarantee that you will be content with yourself. Therefore, you should not shift the burden of your discontent on your partner since doing so often leads to misunderstandings in couples relationships.

You and your partner have a natural propensity to influence and be affected by one another; nevertheless, you need to find a way to transcend this inclination, hunt for happiness inside yourself, and look for it in your relationship or marriage.

Give each other support and encouragement. It is essential for both partners in a marriage to express their love and support for one another, especially in public settings. Always remember that your spouse looks up to you and craves the love and support of your undivided attention at all times.

If you want your marriage to be happy, you need to learn how to support even your partner's most minor efforts, whether inside the family or outside of it. If you want your marriage to be happy, you must learn how to support your partner's most minor efforts.

Don't Try to Bring About Change or Be a Pesterer. Try not make the mistake of attempting to force your will on your partner or expecting them to become the person you envision for them. Because everyone has their way of doing things, it is to your best advantage to show support and trust in the decisions that other people make on your behalf.

Nagging! If you want to be happy in any relationship, including your marriage, you must avoid petty disputes and the continual nagging that goes along with them. If you want to be satisfied in any relationship, including your wedding, you must avoid these things.

Do Your Best first time, every time. Set as your daily objective to do the absolute best that you are capable of doing. This also implies that at all times, we should treat one another with respect, decency, gentleness, compassion, warmth, and sensitivity.

Treat your partner or spouse as a distinct person like you did before you were married or began dating. This will help you keep the same attitude toward them that you had before you got married or started dating. Get back in charge of such situations so you may regain the pleasure you and your partner used to experience.

These were the essential aspects of a married life that contributed to one's level of happiness. At this point, I do not doubt that you are aware of the aspects that lead to a good marriage and how a happy marriage may be achieved. I feel that this video offering advice on how to be content in a marriage would be something that you would find to be of great interest and to which you would feel a connection.

About The Author

Dheeraj Mehrotra, MS, MPhil, PhD (Education Management) honoris causa., a white and a yellow belt in SIX SIGMA, a Certified NLP Business Diploma holder, is an Educational Innovator, Author, with expertise in Six Sigma In Education, Academic Audits, Neuro-Linguistic Programming (NLP), Total Quality Management In Education, an Experiential Educator, a CBSE Resource towards School Assessment (SQAA), CCE, JIT, Five S, and KAIZEN. He has authored over 100 books on topics which include Computer Science, AI, Digital Body Language, NLP, Quality Circles, School Management, Classroom Effectiveness and Safety and security in schools. A former Principal at De Indian Public School, New Delhi, (INDIA), NPS International School, Guwahati, and Education Officer at GEMS, Gurgaon, with an ample teaching experience of over Two Decades, he is a certified Trainer for Quality Circles/ TQM in Education and QCI Standards for School Accreditation/ School Audits and Management. He has also been honoured with the President of India's National Teacher Award in the year 2006 and the Best Science Teacher State Award (By the Ministry of Science and Technology, State of UP), Innovation in Education for his inception of Six Sigma In Education by Education Watch, New Delhi and Education World- Best Teacher Award, BOLT Learner Teacher Award by Air India, 'Innovation in Education Award 2016' by Higher Education Forum (HEF), Gujarat Chapter, among others.

He has developed over 150 FREE EDUCATIONAL MOBILE Apps for the Google Play Store exclusively for Teachers, Students, and Parents. This work has been recognised by the LIMCA BOOK OF RECORDS & INDIA BOOK OF RECORDS as the only Indian to draw that feast. Dr Mehrotra works as a PRINCIPAL at KUNWARS GLOBAL SCHOOL, Lucknow, in India. He has conducted over 1000 workshops globally on "Excellence In Education" integrated with Total Quality Management and Six Sigma, Technology Integration in Education (TIE), Developing towards being ROCKSTAR TEACHERS, including Cyberspace, Cyber Security, Classroom Management, School Leadership & Management, and Innovative teaching within classrooms via Mind Maps, NLP and Experiential Learning in Academics. He is an active TEDx speaker and can be viewed on the youtube TEDx channel.

As a premium UDEMY Instructor, he has developed over 450 courses and caters to over 8 Lakh students from 180 countries.

He can be visited at www.authordheerajmehrotra.com.

References

Books By The Same Author

Disruptive
Literacy
Dr Dheeraj Mehrotra

BY NATIONAL
AWARDEE
EDUCATOR
Teaching in the VUCA WORLD
Kindle Price: ₹ 72.00
inclusive of all taxes
Dr. Dheeraj Mehrotra
authordheerajmehrotra.com
Flipkart
available at
amazon

BY NATIONAL
AWARDEE
EDUCATOR
M.R.P.: ₹ 299.00
Buy New: ₹ 268.00
Save ₹ 31.00 (10%)
inclusive of all taxes
SECURING SAFETY & QUALITY CARING
99 SAFETY AND
SECURITY
ANCHORS WITHIN SCHOOLS
DR. DHEERAJ MEHROTRA
authordheerajmehrotra.com
Flipkart
available at
amazon

9 798889 355861

Printed by Libri Plureos GmbH in Hamburg, Germany